Fact Finders®

MEDIA LITERACY

# Virtually True

## Questioning Online Media

by Guofang Wan

Capstone press®

Mankato, Minnesota

Fact Finders is published by Capstone Press,
151 Good Counsel Drive, P.O. Box 669, Mankato, Minnesota 56002.
www.capstonepress.com

*Library of Congress Cataloging-in-Publication Data*
Wan, Guofang.
   Virtually true : questioning online media / by Guofang Wan.
   p. cm. —(Fact finders. Media literacy)
   Summary: "Describes what media is, how the Internet is part of media, and encourages readers to question the medium's influential messages"—Provided by publisher.
   Includes bibliographical references and index.
   ISBN-13: 978-0-7368-6767-2 (hardcover)
   ISBN-10: 0-7368-6767-8 (hardcover)
   ISBN-13: 978-0-7368-7863-0 (softcover pbk.)
   ISBN-10: 0-7368-7863-7 (softcover pbk.)
   1. Electronic information resource literacy—Juvenile literature. 2. Internet literacy—Juvenile literature. 3. Mass media and children—Juvenile literature. 4. Truthfulness and falsehood—Juvenile literature.  I. Title. II. Title: Questioning online media.
ZA4201.W35 2007
025.04—dc22                                                              2006021446

**Editorial Credits**
Jennifer Besel, editor; Juliette Peters, designer; Jo Miller, photo researcher/photo editor

**Photo Credits**
AP/Wide World Photos/Elise Amendola, 28 (bottom)
Capstone Press/Karon Dubke, 4 (all), 6 (all), 7 (all), 8 (all), 9 (all), 10 (all), 11 (all), 12 (all), 13, 14 (all), 15, 16 (all), 18 (all), 19 (all), 20 (all), 21, 22, 23, 25, 26, 27 (all), 29 (all)
Courtesy of Guofang Wan, 32
Getty Images Inc./AFP/Craig Lassig, 17
Photo Courtesy of Leonard Kleinrock, 28 (top)
Shutterstock/Chin Kit Sen, cover (mouse); fred goldstein, cover (TV); Sebastian Kaulitzki, (background) 17, 21, 23

The author would like to dedicate this book to her daughter, Melissa, for showing her how children surf online.

# TABLE OF CONTENTS

Surfing the Media ......................................... 4

Contact the Webmaster ............................. 6

Sign Our Guestbook ................................... 12

Values Home Page ....................................... 14

What'sMissing.com ..................................... 18

Congrats! You've Won a Prize! ................. 24

Time Line ........................................................ 28

Glossary ........................................................... 30

Internet Sites ................................................ 31

Read More ...................................................... 31

Index ................................................................. 32

Meet the Author ........................................... 32

# Surfing the Media

Where do you look when you need information? Books? Newspapers? How about the Internet? Each of these sources is a way to communicate an idea. And they're all a part of the **media**.

One big piece of the media is the Internet. Most of us couldn't go a single day without using it. The Internet gives us information and entertainment. It also gives us ideas.

Because it's such a huge part of our lives, the Internet also **influences** us. The messages on the Web try to tell us what to think, how to act, and how to feel. That's why questioning what we see and hear is so important. Try asking these questions the next time you hop online.

## QUESTION IT!

**Who made the message and why?**

**Who is the message for?**

**How might others view the message differently?**

**What is left out of the message?**

**How does the message get and keep my attention?**

## Who made the message and why?

People put sites on the Web so they can communicate with millions of people. What other medium offers such a huge audience? **Promoting** goods and ideas has never been easier.

For some Web sites, the goal is to get even more **consumers**. Sites like Target.com allow people who don't live near a Target to shop at the store. Smaller stores also benefit from online shoppers. Without the Web, these stores might never have been able to promote their products worldwide.

Whether they are big or small, businesses use the Internet to promote their products or services.

## LINGO

**webmaster:** the person who designs, develops, markets, or maintains a Web site

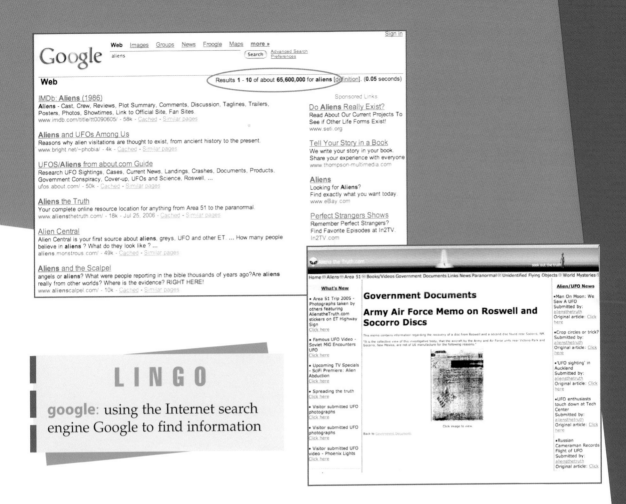

**LINGO**

**google:** using the Internet search engine Google to find information

## Need an Idea?

Other sites are created to promote an idea to people who are looking for an answer. Google the word "aliens" and you'll get at least 65 million hits. Many of those sites are trying to sell the idea of an alien cover-up in the government.

## Database Search

You've probably heard of a database before. But what is it? Well, a database is a collection of articles, journals, and other published materials that all relate to one large topic. A few companies, like LexisNexis and Westlaw, realized that they could make money by organizing information for people. These companies charge a subscription fee to users. But in exchange, users get reliable information about topics they're looking for. Most of what you'll find in a database has been checked by editors.

## Contact Information

It's not always easy to find out who made a site. But knowing who made a site helps you know how reliable the message is. Say you're looking for info on ways to get rid of a headache. If you see that a doctor from the Center for Headache Research wrote the article you're reading, you can be more confident that the info is trustworthy.

Take a look at these two sites about chameleons. Can you find who made them? Hint: Sometimes looking under the "Contact" section will lead you to the answer.

- Chameleon Care and Information Center:
  http://chamaeleonidae.com
- Chameleons Online:
  http://www.chameleonsonline.com

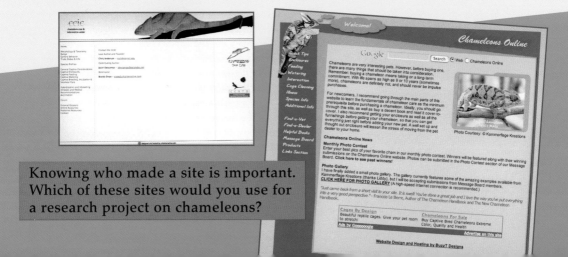

Knowing who made a site is important. Which of these sites would you use for a research project on chameleons?

All kinds of people make Web sites. And they make them for different reasons. Here are just a few.

**COMPANIES** create databases to make researching easier and to make money.

**NEWSPAPERS** put their papers online to reach more readers.

**MOVIE STUDIOS** create Web sites to promote a new movie.

**STORES** put their products online so we can buy them without having to get out of our pajamas.

**SCHOOL CLASSES** put their projects on the Web so parents can view them.

The **GOVERNMENT** puts forms and other information on their Web site. Then people can **access** the things they need.

Many **PEOPLE** make personal sites or blogs to share their thoughts.

# Sign Our Guestbook

## Who is the message for?

Webmasters create Web sites in order to reach a lot of people. But that doesn't mean they think everyone will be interested. Every site is made for a specific target audience. A site like pbskids.org is made for kids. But www.irs.gov is for tax-paying adults.

## LINGO

**adware:** software that is attached to another program; adware pops up banner ads.

**spyware:** software that tracks a user's Web activities without his or her knowledge

**target audience:** the group of people that marketers think will be interested in their message

Webmasters and **marketers** do things to learn about their target audience. One way to get this info is to attach adware or spyware to downloadable programs. This software collects data about what you do online.

Other sites send cookies to your computer. And we're not talking about chocolate chip ones. These cookies are written to your hard drive and they remember your passwords for you. But sites use cookies for other reasons too. They can use the cookies to track where you go and what you do on a site. By doing this, site makers learn what you like. They use that info to attract more people like you.

E-mail sites, like Yahoo! Mail, often offer to remember your password. Just know if you click the box, you just might be accepting cookies too.

# Values Home Page

## How might others view the message differently?

You have your favorite Web sites, right? But did you know that your age, gender, life experiences, and even your religious beliefs affect what you like about a site? That's why you might enjoy Nick.com but your mom is checking out Parent.com.

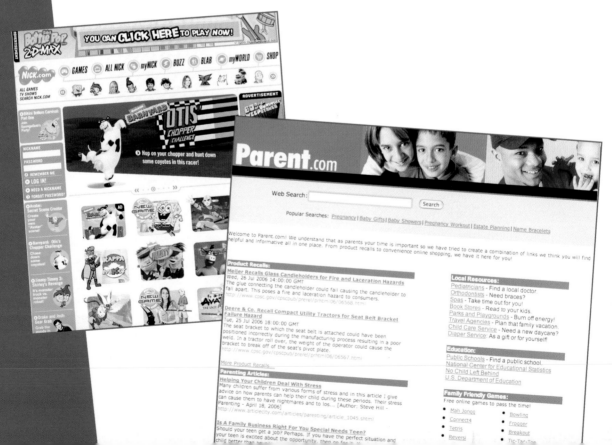

Your values, or what you think is important, help you decide what sites are true, funny, or **offensive**. One thing to keep in mind is that everyone has different values. A site that is funny to you might be offensive to someone else.

Although this online game is supposed to be funny, some people might find it offensive.

# TRY IT OUT!

You can make a Web page that tries to influence people to think like you do. Grab a piece of paper and jot down what values you want to promote on your site. Here are some questions to help you decide what to talk about.

- What do you hate?
- What do you really believe in?
- What is something you love?

Use the answer to one or all of these questions to draw up a Web page. You could try to convince people that cats can fly—if that's what you believe!

## *Values.com*

Web sites are filled with values. Webmasters have their own thoughts and feelings, and they put those beliefs in their sites. As you surf the Net, ideas are everywhere. Apple.com tells you the hottest music to put on your iPod. Sites like Gap.com try to influence you to buy their products. The Net is a great place to get and share ideas. Just remember you can always question the ideas you're getting and make your own decisions.

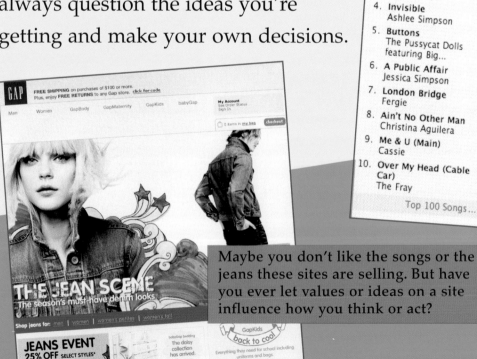

**iTunes Top Songs**

1. Crazy
   Gnarls Barkley
2. Deja Vu (Featuring Jay-Z)
   Beyoncé featuring Jay-Z
3. Promiscuous
   Nelly Furtado & Timbaland
4. Invisible
   Ashlee Simpson
5. Buttons
   The Pussycat Dolls featuring Big...
6. A Public Affair
   Jessica Simpson
7. London Bridge
   Fergie
8. Ain't No Other Man
   Christina Aguilera
9. Me & U (Main)
   Cassie
10. Over My Head (Cable Car)
    The Fray

Top 100 Songs...

Maybe you don't like the songs or the jeans these sites are selling. But have you ever let values or ideas on a site influence how you think or act?

# Reality Check

The Internet is a great place to spread values to a whole lot of people. Politicians have taken note. The 1998 race for Minnesota governor was the first time online campaigning really proved how powerful it could be. Former pro wrestler Jesse Ventura decided to run for governor. Ventura, a member of the Reform Party, had little support and even less money. All he had was an e-mail list and a Web site. Using this technology, Ventura spread his campaign messages. With the help of his online campaign, he won half the votes from people under 30 years old. These votes were a major reason Ventura won the seat as governor of Minnesota.

## What is left out of the message?

Since nobody is out there making sure sites have correct info, we have to do it ourselves. One good place to start is by asking, "What's left out?"

Information like who made the site, when it was updated, and where they got their facts should be on a Web site. But some sites leave that information out. Why? Who knows. But if it's not there, be careful.

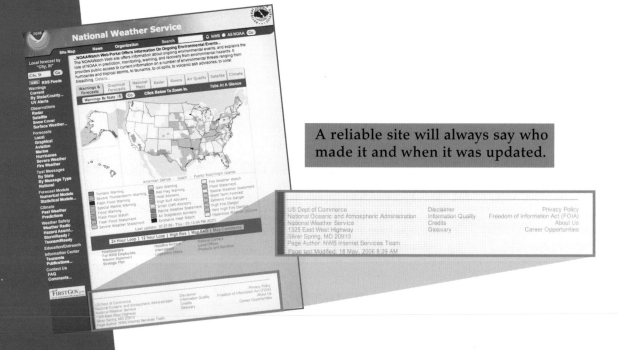

A reliable site will always say who made it and when it was updated.

## No Answers Matched Your Search

Check out this site:

www.nasa.gov/audience/forkids

At the bottom of each page you see who the editor was. You can also see who checked the info, and when it was last updated. That's great. You can be more confident that the info there is going to be correct.

Now check out this site about space:

www.kidsastronomy.com

Look around on this page. Can you find info about who made it? There isn't anything saying where they got their info or when it was updated. This site might be fun to look at, but should you use it for your science report?

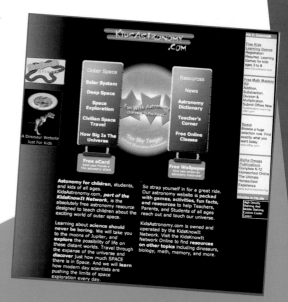

## Fake Web Site Here

Some webmasters leave out pieces of info about who made the site. But others leave out more than that. Some Web site makers just happen to leave out the fact that their Web sites are completely fake. Take a look at the Web site about the dangers of Dihydrogen Monoxide, www.dhmo.org.

This site looks pretty official, doesn't it? But Dihydrogen Monoxide isn't dangerous. It's just plain old water. Were you fooled?

Sometimes it's hard to tell if the info on a site is real or not. Take a look at the Mike the Headless Chicken site, www.miketheheadless chicken.org.

Do you think this site is true or not? Look for information about who made the site and where they got their info. Also, dig around online to double-check the info.

20

# Reality Check

In 2003, three boys from Akron, Ohio, decided to make a Web site. But they didn't make just any site. Their site looked just like the real news site CNN.com. The difference was that the boys' site had stories about fake events. One story said that Dave Matthews of the Dave Matthews Band had died. Another reported that the Olsen twins would be attending college at Notre Dame.

Even though it had many spelling and grammar mistakes, the fake CNN site fooled thousands of people. Even some newspapers and TV stations reported the stories from the site as news. Too bad they didn't question the site before using it.

The fake CNN news site looked a lot like the real CNN site shown here. It's not always easy to tell real from fake in the virtual world.

## Check Sources

No one really owns the Net, so anyone can make a Web site. That's really cool. But it can also be a problem. You see, since no one is checking the facts it can be hard to know if the information is really correct. Knowing who made a site, why the site was made, and who the site is for can really help you decide if a site is reliable. Checking sites for values and missing info is a great way to find out if the message is true, false, or in between.

Always remember to double- and triple-check the information you get online. Books, magazines, and databases are good places to check info. If you see a fact in many sources, it's more likely to be correct.

Your computer isn't the only place to find answers. Using other sources, like magazines and books, will help you find great information too.

# Reality Check

We can't believe everything we read on the Net. No one knows this better than John Seigenthaler Sr. from Nashville, Tennessee. In May 2005, Seigenthaler read about himself in the online encyclopedia Wikipedia. He was surprised to find that someone wrote that he had been involved with the shootings of both President John F. Kennedy and Senator Robert Kennedy. That simply was not true.

Wikipedia allows anyone to change info in an article or add articles of their own. The problem is that there are no fact checkers on Wikipedia. So errors, and even jokes like this one, do happen. Just goes to show that when anyone can post, the information might be bad.

## LINGO

**post**: putting an entry on a blog or an Internet forum

23

# Congrats! You've Won a Prize!

## How does the message get and keep my attention?

You are the winner! Click here for your free laptop!

Ever gotten a message like that? Getting a free laptop would be pretty cool. (The word "free" gets us every time.) So you click onto the site. And the trick has worked again! Pop-up ads are just one of the many ways Web site makers grab your attention. The promise of free downloads or contests gets us to click onto a site. And that's what site makers want. They can't influence you if you're not looking.

**CONGRATULATIONS!**
You've won a free laptop computer!
Click here to **Claim Your Prize!**

There are so many sites online that Web sites have to make a good first impression. If they don't, you'll move on. So their pages are filled with bright colors, animations, and cool pics. These tricks get you interested in the site, so you'll stick around.

This site for the movie *Over the Hedge* is bright and fun. Would it get your attention?

Getting people interested in a site isn't easy. Grab some paper, markers, and even some magazines lying around the house. Pretend your paper is a Web site. Create a fun site that people will be attracted to. Use these questions to help you get started.

- Who do I want to look at my site?
- What things will draw people to my site?
- Will there be pop-up ads? If so, what will they say?

## Try This!

Once a site has your attention, it has to keep it. So Web sites offer all kinds of things to do. Chat rooms get people talking to each other. But while you're chatting, don't be surprised to see a few ads pop up or scroll by. Really, the makers of the site wanted you to stay and chat so they could sell you something.

Other attention-keepers are games, music, and shopping. MySpace.com allows people to listen to up-and-coming artists. It's a lot of fun, but there's a catch. MySpace makes money by selling marketers your info. Once these marketers get your info, be prepared for an inbox full of spam.

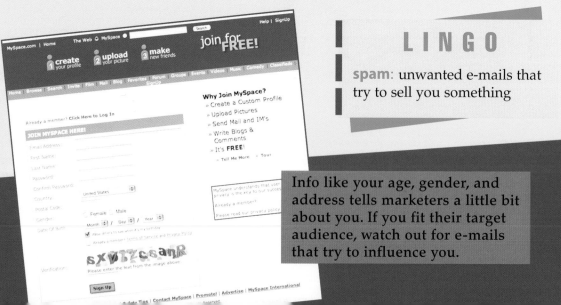

# LINGO

**spam**: unwanted e-mails that try to sell you something

Info like your age, gender, and address tells marketers a little bit about you. If you fit their target audience, watch out for e-mails that try to influence you.

## Search

These days, you can chat with a person from Australia and play chess with someone from China all in one afternoon. With all the people who work and play online come a whole lot of ideas. And that is so cool! But because the Internet is open to everyone, we have to be careful. Not everything on the Web is true. That's why questioning everything is so important. So hop online, do a little surfing, and have fun searching for those little Internet tricks.

# Time Line

The Internet is born. Four universities are connected through computers using a system called ARPAnet.

The word "Internet" is used for the first time.

**1969**  **1972**  **1982**  **1989**

E-mail is introduced.

Tim Berners-Lee develops a way to distribute information on the Net. He calls it the World Wide Web.

Jesse Ventura wins the election for Minnesota governor with the help of e-mail and a Web site, changing the way candidates campaign during elections.

John Seigenthaler Sr. discovers that a Wikipedia article about himself includes untrue info, proving again that information online isn't always correct.

**1998**      **2003**      **2005**

A fake site, that looks much like the real CNN site (shown above), fools thousands of people, proving that questioning info online is important.

# GLOSSARY

**access** (AK-sess)—to get information from a computer

**consumer** (kuhn-SOO-mur)—someone who buys products and services

**influence** (IN-floo-uhnss)—to have an effect on someone or something

**marketer** (MAR-kit-uhr)—a person who sells a product or service

**media** (MEE-dee-uh)—a group of mediums that communicates messages; one piece of the media, like the Internet, is called a medium.

**offensive** (uh-FEN-siv)—causing anger or hurt feelings

**promote** (pruh-MOTE)—to make the public aware of something or someone

**reliable** (ri-LYE-uh-buhl)—trustworthy or dependable

**subscription** (suhb-SKRIP-shun)—a paid membership for a product or service

# INTERNET SITES

FactHound offers a safe, fun way to find Internet sites related to this book. All of the sites on FactHound have been researched by our staff.

Here's how:

1. Visit *www.facthound.com*

2. Choose your grade level.

3. Type in this book ID **0736867678** for age-appropriate sites. You may also browse subjects by clicking on letters, or by clicking on pictures and words.

4. Click on the **Fetch It** button.

**FactHound will fetch the best sites for you!**

## READ MORE

**Ali, Dominic**. *Media Madness: An Insider's Guide to Media*. Tonawanda, N.Y.: Kids Can Press, 2005.

**Morgan, Sally**. *Internet*. Behind Media. Chicago: Heinemann, 2001.

**Pelusey, Michael, and Jane Pelusey**. *Internet*. The Media. Philadelphia: Chelsea House, 2005.

# INDEX

adware, 12
attention-getting tricks,
    24, 25
attention-keeping tricks, 26

chat rooms, 26, 27
cookies, 13

databases, 8, 10, 22

fake Web sites, 20, 21

Google, 7

influence, 5, 15, 16, 24

marketers, 12, 26
media, 4, 6
missing information, 18–19,
    20, 21, 22, 23
MySpace, 26

politics and the Internet, 17
pop-up ads, 12, 24, 25, 26

Seigenthaler, John, Sr., 23
spyware, 12

target audiences, 12, 26

values, 15, 16, 17, 22
Ventura, Jesse, 17

webmasters, 6, 12, 16, 20
who makes sites, 8–9,
    10, 11, 12, 18, 19, 20, 22
why sites are made, 6, 7, 8–9,
    10, 12, 22
Wikipedia, 23

# MEET THE AUTHOR

Dr. Guofang Wan teaches future teachers at Ohio University. She is a big fan of teaching children with and about multimedia. Her other book, *The Media-Savvy Student*, and her many journal articles help to bring media literacy into the classroom.